First Edition, 2026 | United States of America

Disclaimer: This book is for educational and informational purposes only and does not constitute financial, investment, tax, or legal advice. Cryptocurrency involves significant risk. Always consult qualified professionals before making investment decisions.

All statistics and platform information are accurate as of June 2025. The cryptocurrency landscape changes rapidly — always verify current information before acting.

ISBN 978-1-948613-35-4

Library of Congress Control Number: 2026945267

Printed in the United States of America

Sunny Day Publishing, LLC
Cuyahoga Falls, Ohio 44223
www.sunnydaypublishing.com
editor@sunnydaypublishing.com

Crypto Without Confusion

A Real Investor's Step-by-Step Guide to Wallets, Trading, and Staying Safe

---

Shelley Kimberly

Featured contributor in The Power of Mentorship series

About the Author

Shelley Kimberly is a published contributor in *The Power of Mentorship* series, where her work appears alongside globally recognized leaders such as Zig Ziglar, Jim Rohn, Denis Waitley, Brian Tracy, Marie Diamond, Bob Proctor, Chris Widener, Greg Reid, Edward James Olmos, Vic Johnson, Hasnain Khaku, and Glen Curry. She was also featured in the special edition *The Power of Mentorship: The Law of Attraction*, appearing alongside Marie Diamond, one of the featured teachers in the worldwide phenomenon *The Secret*.

Her curiosity and drive to simplify complex ideas led her into the world of cryptocurrency, where she has spent years learning how to navigate wallets, exchanges, decentralized platforms, and tokenomics. She brings the same clear, empowering voice to this book, breaking down intimidating concepts into simple, actionable steps for everyday readers.

Shelley enjoys a balanced lifestyle centered on family, which she considers her greatest joy. She has been married for over 30 years and raised three amazing kids. She is a colon cancer survivor and feels blessed to be healthy now. She also enjoys attending Cleveland Browns and Cleveland Cavaliers games, and following her alma mater, The Ohio State University, especially during football season.

Contents

Introduction

Before investing in cryptocurrency, it is essential to **do your own research (DYOR)**. Unlike traditional assets such as stocks or bonds, cryptocurrencies are intangible digital assets, and you can purchase fractional amounts rather than whole units. While the crypto market is notoriously volatile and carries significant risks, it also holds tremendous potential for profit.

My own journey into crypto has been shaped by countless hours of learning through online resources such as CoinMarketCap, Investopedia, Coinbase, and Crypto.com. Among these, CoinMarketCap has been indispensable, providing up-to-the-minute data on thousands of assets. Founded in 2013, it has become one of the most trusted and unbiased price-tracking platforms, often cited by CNBC and Bloomberg. I have also connected with fellow enthusiasts on Telegram, X, and Discord — communities that offered unique perspectives and helped demystify the crypto world.

I do not claim to be an expert, but I understand the intimidation many newcomers feel when first entering this space. That is why I wrote this book — not to tell you what to buy, but to provide a **foundation that equips you with the tools and confidence** to explore crypto on your own.

Quick Tips Before You Dive In

Here are key factors to evaluate when deciding whether a cryptocurrency is worth investing in:

- **White Paper:** Outlines the project's purpose, technology, and roadmap. A solid white paper reveals how serious the team is.

- **Utility & Value Proposition:** What problem does this project solve? How is it useful in the real world?
- **Development Team:** Are the team members publicly known ("doxxed") or anonymous? Transparent teams inspire more trust.
- **Market Cap & Blockchain:** Market capitalization shows the project's size and stability; the blockchain reveals its scalability and security.
- **Community & Presence:** Strong social media engagement, a professional website, and active supporters often signal credibility.

My First Steps Into Cryptocurrency

I was first introduced to cryptocurrency in 2017. My journey began with Coinbase, a beginner-friendly exchange. On December 15, 2017, I made my very first purchase: Litecoin (LTC). That single trade sparked my interest, and soon I was experimenting with other assets, including Shiba Inu and several altcoins.

My real breakthrough came in December 2021, when I ventured into decentralized exchanges (DEXs). Unlike centralized platforms, a DEX allows users to trade directly through smart contracts, without a central authority. One of the first DEXs I used was PancakeSwap, built on the Binance Smart Chain, which uses an Automated Market Maker (AMM) to set prices and execute trades.

The Early Days of Cryptocurrency

As of 2024, about 6.8% of the global population — over 560 million people — own some form of cryptocurrency. That is a small fraction of the world's population, meaning adoption is still in its early stages. If you are reading this, you have not "missed the boat."

A Note on Repetition

You may notice some ideas revisited in different chapters. This is intentional. Repetition reinforces the most important points so you not only read them but truly absorb their meaning. Reviewing key concepts from multiple angles helps the information stick.

CHAPTER 1

Chapter 1 — The History of Money, Bitcoin & Satoshi Nakamoto

Money has taken many forms throughout history. Ancient societies relied on barter, exchanging goods and services directly. Over time, barter gave way to commodity money — gold, silver, and salt. As trade expanded, paper money and banking systems emerged, where trust was placed in governments and financial institutions. The 2008 global financial crisis exposed many flaws in traditional finance. Out of this moment, Bitcoin was born.

Who Is Satoshi Nakamoto?

The story of cryptocurrency starts with Satoshi Nakamoto, the mysterious inventor of Bitcoin. No one knows whether Nakamoto is a single individual or a group of people, and their true identity remains unconfirmed. The pseudonym is Japanese in origin, but most experts believe Nakamoto may not actually be Japanese.

Timeline of Key Events

- **May 2007:** Nakamoto began coding the first version of Bitcoin.
- **August 18, 2008:** The domain bitcoin.org was registered.
- **October 31, 2008:** Nakamoto published the white paper "Bitcoin: A Peer-to-Peer Electronic Cash System."
- **January 3, 2009:** Nakamoto mined the genesis block, officially launching the network. Embedded in the code: "The Times 03/Jan/2009 Chancellor on brink of second bailout for banks."
- **May 2010:** Two pizzas were famously purchased for 10,000 BTC — a reminder of how far crypto has come.
- **2010:** Nakamoto ceased public involvement with Bitcoin.

Bitcoin's Three Revolutionary Ideas

- **Decentralization:** No central authority controls the network.
- **Scarcity:** Only 21 million Bitcoin will ever exist.

- **Transparency:** All transactions are permanently recorded on the blockchain.

■ Action Plan — 3 Things You Can Do Today

1. Read Satoshi Nakamoto's Bitcoin White Paper (available free online). Highlight one concept you did not understand for further study.
2. Look up the Genesis Block message and reflect on its meaning in the context of the 2008 financial crisis.
3. Make a timeline: barter → gold → banks → digital → Bitcoin. This will anchor your understanding.

CHAPTER 2

Chapter 2 — What Exactly Is Cryptocurrency?

The word "cryptocurrency" is rooted in cryptography, derived from the Greek word *kryptos* meaning "hidden." Cryptography refers to secure methods of encrypting and decrypting information. Cryptocurrency uses these principles to enable secure digital transactions that only the sender and receiver can verify.

Unlike dollars or euros, cryptocurrency exists only in digital form. It is created through computer code and cryptographic protocols that secure transactions and govern the creation of new units.

Key Features of Cryptocurrency

- **Irreversibility:** Once confirmed, transactions cannot be undone. Double-check wallet addresses before every send.
- **Decentralization:** No bank, government, or single entity controls cryptocurrencies.
- **Privacy:** Transactions are pseudonymous, secured by private keys.
- **Blockchain Technology:** Transactions are grouped into blocks, linked in a chain, and verified by a distributed network of computers. Once recorded, data cannot be altered.

You do not need to understand every technical detail — just like most people do not fully understand the banking system but can still use a debit card. What matters is that crypto gives you a new way to store, send, and spend value digitally.

■ Action Plan — 3 Things You Can Do Today

1. Download a crypto wallet app (Coinbase Wallet, MetaMask, or Trust Wallet). Don't buy yet — just explore the interface.
2. Visit CoinMarketCap or CoinGecko and check today's top 10 cryptocurrencies. Note how they differ in market cap, purpose, and utility.
3. Write down one personal reason why cryptocurrency interests you. This will help guide your learning journey.

CHAPTER 3

Chapter 3 — Hot and Cold Wallets

Securing your cryptocurrency is essential to protect against potential loss or theft. Here are key strategies to keep your assets safe.

1. Use a Crypto Wallet

A crypto wallet is a secure tool for storing cryptocurrency. It holds your digital assets, private keys, and wallet addresses — similar to a digital safety deposit box. Examples include Trust Wallet, Coinbase Wallet, and Ledger Nano X.

2. Choose the Right Wallet Type

A **hot wallet** (like Trust Wallet or MetaMask) is connected to the internet, offering quick access. When setting up a hot wallet, you will receive a recovery seed phrase — store it securely, for your eyes only.

A **cold wallet** is kept offline and offers higher security. Hardware wallets such as Ledger Nano X, Trezor Model T, and SafePal S1 are popular cold wallet options.

3. Consider Using an Exchange

You may also store cryptocurrency on an exchange. Although convenient, exchanges are more vulnerable to cyber attacks. Choose a reputable exchange: Crypto.com, Kraken, or Coinbase.

4. Secure Your Recovery Phrase

Keep a physical copy of your wallet's recovery phrase in a safe location. Tools specifically designed for this include the CryptoSteel Capsule, Billfodl, Cobo Tablet, and SafePal CypherSeed Board.

■ Action Plan — 3 Things You Can Do Today

1. Research hot and cold wallets — look at Coinbase Wallet and Ledger Nano X and compare their features.
2. Look up a crypto exchange such as Coinbase and review its security features.
3. Set up a hot wallet and write down your recovery phrase in a dedicated, secure location.

CHAPTER 4

Chapter 4 — Real-Life Crypto Utility and Core Concepts

Section 1: Decentralized Finance (DeFi) and Lending

DeFi lending allows people to lend and borrow digital assets without relying on banks. These platforms operate on blockchain networks and are powered by smart contracts — self-executing digital agreements that automatically enforce terms once specific conditions are met.

Real-Life Example: Aave Lending

1. **Creating an Account –** Matt, an ETH holder, connects his MetaMask wallet to Aave.
2. **Depositing ETH –** Matt deposits ETH into a liquidity pool that borrowers can access.
3. **Earning Interest –** As borrowers pay interest, Matt earns a share based on the amount he deposited.
4. **Borrowing Assets –** Matt borrows USDC stablecoin by locking his ETH as collateral.
5. **Repaying the Loan –** Once Matt repays his loan plus interest, his ETH collateral is released.

Section 2: Stablecoins vs. Non-Stable Cryptocurrencies

- **Stablecoins:** Pegged to assets like USD, keeping their value consistent. Examples: USDT, USDC, DAI.
- **Non-stable cryptocurrencies:** Such as Bitcoin, fluctuate dramatically — higher profit potential and higher risk.

Types of Stablecoins

- **Fiat-backed:** Supported by traditional currency reserves — USDT, USDC.

- **Crypto-backed:** Collateralized with other cryptocurrencies — DAI.
- **Algorithmic:** Use algorithms to balance supply and demand — Ampleforth.

Section 3: Coins vs. Tokens

Coins are native to their own blockchain (e.g., Bitcoin). Tokens are created with a smart contract on existing blockchains like Ethereum. The six primary token types are:

- **Utility Tokens:** Grant access to a platform's products or services — Chainlink ($LINK), Binance Coin ($BNB).
- **Security Tokens:** Represent real-world assets like company shares — $XYO, $AMP.
- **Transactional Tokens:** Used primarily as currency within a network.
- **Platform Tokens:** Support dApps and other functionalities within blockchain platforms.
- **Governance Tokens:** Allow holders to vote on protocol updates or community fund allocations.
- **Non-Fungible Tokens (NFTs):** Represent unique digital items that are non-interchangeable.

Section 4: Keys and Seed Phrases

Private Key

The private key is a unique string acting like a password for your cryptocurrency wallet. It is the only way to access and authorize transactions. Losing it means losing access to your assets permanently.

Recovery Seed Phrase

The recovery seed phrase represents your private key as a human-readable list of 12–24 words. Every time you create a new wallet, write down the seed phrase exactly as given and store it securely offline.

Critical Warning

The recovery seed phrase is the only way to recover your assets if your wallet is compromised. Store it offline in a safe, fireproof, waterproof location. No support team can assist you if you lose it.

■ Action Plan — 3 Things You Can Do Today

1. Search hot and cold crypto wallets — look at MetaMask, Trust Wallet, Ledger Nano X, and Trezor Model T.
2. Search out a few tokens and coins — examples: USDC (stablecoin), Bitcoin, PEPE.
3. Buy a dedicated journal to keep your seed phrases safe (the notes section at the end of this book also works).

CHAPTER 5

Chapter 5 — NFTs and the Metaverse

An NFT, or non-fungible token, is a type of digital asset that represents ownership of a unique item, recorded and verified on a blockchain. Non-fungible means each NFT is one-of-a-kind and cannot be exchanged equally with another. NFTs can represent digital art, GIFs, video clips, sports highlights, collectibles, virtual avatars, video game assets, and music.

How to Purchase an NFT

1. **A Crypto Wallet** – Compatible with the blockchain hosting the NFT. Popular free options: Coinbase Wallet, Binance Wallet.
2. **Funds** – If the NFT is on Ethereum, you will need Ether (ETH), purchasable on exchanges like Coinbase.
3. **An NFT Marketplace** – Leading options: OpenSea, Rarible, Coinbase NFT. Connect your wallet and browse.

Keep in mind that all transactions typically incur **gas fees**, which you will need to pay even if the NFT itself is free.

The Metaverse Connection

The metaverse describes a shared, persistent digital universe where people interact using avatars. It blends social media, gaming, VR, and AR. The metaverse is not one single platform — it is a network of virtual worlds powered by blockchain technology.

- **Digital Identity:** Avatars can wear NFT-based clothing or accessories, creating a unique online identity.
- **Virtual Real Estate:** Platforms like Decentraland and The Sandbox let users buy NFT plots of land.
- **Economic Layer:** NFTs function as tradeable assets within the metaverse economy.
- **Cross-Platform Ownership:** Because NFTs exist on blockchains, they are not confined to one platform.

■ Action Plan — 3 Things You Can Do Today

1. Explore a metaverse platform like Decentraland, The Sandbox, or Spatial.
2. Research NFT marketplaces (e.g., OpenSea, Magic Eden) to see how digital items are bought and sold.
3. Consider creating a simple NFT (like a digital image) to understand how ownership transfers on the blockchain.

CHAPTER 6

Chapter 6 — Smart Contracts, P2P Transactions & Exchanges

Smart Contracts

A smart contract is a self-executing agreement where the terms are written directly into computer code. Running on blockchains like Ethereum, smart contracts automatically enforce rules once specific conditions are met — without lawyers, banks, or other intermediaries. Smart contracts power DeFi, NFTs, supply chains, voting systems, and in-game ownership.

Cryptocurrency Exchanges

The easiest way to buy cryptocurrency is through an **exchange** — a digital marketplace for buying, selling, and trading crypto. Popular exchanges include Coinbase, Gemini, Kraken, and Binance. Always use reputable platforms and follow strong security practices such as two-factor authentication.

Peer-to-Peer (P2P) Transactions

At its core, cryptocurrency is **peer-to-peer (P2P)** — individuals interact directly without going through banks. Every participant (or node) has equal authority. Transactions are validated collectively rather than by a single authority, reducing fraud and eliminating middlemen.

Centralized vs. Decentralized Exchanges

- **Centralized Exchanges (CEXs):** Platforms like Coinbase make it easy to buy crypto with fiat money. Beginner-friendly but hold custody of your funds.
- **Decentralized Exchanges (DEXs):** Platforms like PancakeSwap, Uniswap, or Raydium allow direct wallet-to-wallet trades. Often list newer tokens early but require more technical know-how.

A common strategy: **use CEXs for simplicity and DEXs for opportunities**. Start with a CEX, then branch out to DEXs once you are more comfortable.

■ Action Plan — 3 Things You Can Do Today

1. Open an account on a trusted exchange (like Coinbase or Kraken) and complete the verification process.
2. Fund your account and send a small test transaction to a friend or second wallet to experience P2P payments firsthand.
3. Research one dApp (decentralized application) like Uniswap, PancakeSwap, or Raydium.

CHAPTER 7

Chapter 7 — The Solana Ecosystem: How Phantom Makes Crypto Simple

Phantom is a self-custodial crypto wallet built primarily for the Solana ecosystem. It allows users to store, send, and receive SOL and Solana-based tokens, and it integrates directly with decentralized apps (dApps) on the network. One of Phantom's defining features is its built-in ability to purchase crypto through third-party payment providers, letting users fund their wallet with fiat currency using methods such as debit cards, Apple Pay, PayPal, or bank transfers. These purchases are processed externally, and the tokens are delivered straight to the user's wallet once the provider completes the transaction.

Phantom is available as both a mobile app and a browser extension. When a new wallet is empty, the interface highlights options to add funds, either by buying SOL directly or by receiving tokens from another wallet or exchange. The wallet automatically displays the correct deposit address and warns users to ensure they are using the correct network to avoid loss of funds.

Solana, SOL, and the Solana Exchange Landscape

Solana is a high-performance blockchain designed for fast, low-cost transactions. Its native token, SOL, is used for transaction fees, staking, and interacting with applications built on the network.

People typically acquire SOL through two main avenues:

- **Centralized Exchanges (CEXs):** Binance, Coinbase, and Kraken offer regulated environments and fiat on-ramps for beginners.
- **Decentralized Exchanges (DEXs):** Built on Solana — including Raydium, Orca, and Jupiter — these allow wallet-to-wallet trading without intermediaries.

Phantom integrates seamlessly with these DEXs, making it possible to trade SOL and other Solana tokens directly inside the wallet interface.

Why Phantom and Solana Work So Well Together

The combination of Phantom's user-friendly design and Solana's high-speed infrastructure creates an experience that feels modern, efficient, and accessible. Solana provides the performance foundation, while Phantom delivers the interface that makes the ecosystem easy to navigate. Together, they offer a powerful entry point into decentralized finance — one that balances speed, control, and simplicity.

Buying Crypto Using Phantom and SOL

Step 1: Set Up Your Phantom Wallet

Install Phantom, create a wallet, and store your Secret Recovery Phrase securely. Write it down on paper and keep it offline.

Step 2: Add SOL to Your Wallet

You can fund your wallet in two ways:

A. Buying SOL with Fiat

1. **Open Phantom –** Tap **Buy**.
2. **Select Solana (SOL) –** Choose SOL from the token list.
3. **Enter the amount –** Type the dollar amount you wish to spend.
4. **Choose a payment provider –** Select from the available options (debit card, Apple Pay, PayPal, bank transfer).
5. **Complete the checkout –** SOL appears in your wallet once the provider processes the transaction.

B. Transferring SOL from Another Exchange

1. **Tap Receive –** Open Phantom and tap **Receive**.
2. **Copy your SOL address –** Make sure you are on the Solana network.
3. **Send from your exchange –** Initiate a withdrawal from your exchange account to this address.

Step 3: Swap SOL for Other Tokens

Once your wallet contains SOL:

1. **Open the Swap tab –** Tap **Swap** inside Phantom.
2. **Select SOL –** Choose SOL as the token you want to exchange.
3. **Choose the target token –** Select the token you want to receive.
4. **Review the rate and fee –** Check the exchange rate and any network fee before proceeding.
5. **Confirm the transaction –** The new token appears in your wallet within seconds.

■ Action Plan — 3 Things You Can Do Today

1. Set up Phantom and secure your Secret Recovery Phrase — write it down, store it offline, and never share it with anyone.
2. Fund your wallet with SOL — either buy SOL directly inside Phantom or transfer it from a centralized exchange.
3. Use SOL to make your first swap — open the Swap tab, choose SOL, select your target token, and confirm the transaction.

CHAPTER 8

Chapter 8 — How Cryptocurrency Works: Blockchain Basics & Mining

At the heart of cryptocurrency lies the **blockchain** — a decentralized digital ledger that records every transaction across a network of computers called nodes. Unlike a bank ledger controlled by one institution, a blockchain is maintained collectively.

Blocks and Chains

Transactions are grouped into blocks. Once a block is filled, it is linked to the previous block, forming a chain. Each block contains a list of recent transactions, a timestamp, a cryptographic hash of the previous block, and a unique identifier. This makes the blockchain tamper-resistant: altering any past transaction would break the chain and be immediately rejected.

Mining and Proof of Work (PoW)

Mining refers to using computer power to verify and secure transactions while earning cryptocurrency as a reward. In Bitcoin mining, computers compete to solve a complex mathematical puzzle. The first to succeed adds the block to the blockchain and earns newly generated bitcoins. This competition is called **proof of work**.

Proof of Stake (PoS)

Other cryptocurrencies use Proof of Stake (PoS), where validators are chosen based on how many coins they "stake" (lock up as collateral). This method is more energy-efficient than PoW. Both PoW and PoS rely on **consensus mechanisms** — ways for the network to agree on valid transactions without a central authority.

■ Action Plan — 3 Things You Can Do Today

1. Watch a short video explaining blockchain in under 5 minutes (many simplified versions exist on YouTube).
2. Look up the difference between Proof of Work and Proof of Stake on CoinMarketCap Learn or Ethereum.org. Write down one advantage of each.
3. Track Bitcoin's latest block on blockchain.com to see real-time blockchain activity.

CHAPTER 9

Chapter 9 — What Is a Liquidity Pool?

A liquidity pool is a collection of cryptocurrency funds locked in a smart contract on a DEX. These pools facilitate trading by providing liquidity, allowing users to buy and sell tokens directly from the pool without relying on traditional order books.

Risks: Manipulation and Impermanent Loss

- **Front-Running:** A malicious actor observes a pending transaction and places their own ahead of it to profit from the price change.
- **Impermanent Loss:** Occurs when the value of tokens in the pool fluctuates significantly, leading to potential losses for liquidity providers.

Real-Life Example: Adding Liquidity on Uniswap

1. **Creating an Account** – Caroline, an Ethereum holder, creates an account on Uniswap and connects her MetaMask wallet.
2. **Navigating to the Pool** – She goes to the "Pool" section and selects "Add Liquidity."
3. **Selecting Tokens** – She chooses ETH and USDT, entering the amounts she wants to deposit.
4. **Approving Tokens** – Caroline approves Uniswap to access her tokens in MetaMask (requires a small gas fee).
5. **Adding Liquidity** – Her tokens are deposited. In return, she receives LP tokens representing her share.
6. **Earning Fees** – As traders use the ETH/USDT pool, Caroline earns a portion of trading fees proportional to her share.

■ Action Plan — 3 Things You Can Do Today

1. Find a token on CoinGecko or CoinMarketCap and locate its liquidity pool on Uniswap.
2. Repeat step 1 with a different token to compare pool sizes and trading volumes.
3. If you feel confident, try adding a small amount to a liquidity pool and observe the LP token you receive.

CHAPTER 10

Chapter 10 — Bull vs. Bear: Understanding Market Behavior

Market Cycles

- **Bull Market:** Prices are rising, optimism is high, and investors buy aggressively.
- **Bear Market:** Prices fall, fear dominates, and many investors sell at a loss.

Both cycles are natural. Smart investors do not panic — they adjust strategies.

Common Market Dynamics

- **Volatility:** Crypto prices can swing 10–30% in a single day.
- **Liquidity:** A highly liquid token is safer than one with little trading volume.
- **Community Sentiment:** Memes, social media, and influencers can drive short-term price spikes.
- **Whale Activity:** Large investors buying or selling can move prices dramatically.

The Psychology of Investing

Investor emotions — **FOMO** (fear of missing out) and **FUD** (fear, uncertainty, doubt) — often drive poor decisions: buying at the peak due to hype, selling too early out of panic, or ignoring fundamentals for quick gains. Long-term success comes from discipline, research, and patience.

■ Action Plan — 3 Things You Can Do Today

1. Check a coin's tokenomics on CoinGecko or CoinMarketCap. Look at supply, holders, and utility.
2. Track market sentiment by following a few crypto Twitter/X accounts or Telegram groups.
3. Write down your risk tolerance (e.g., "I can afford to lose $100 without stress") to guide your investing decisions.

CHAPTER 11

Chapter 11 — Risks & Common Mistakes to Avoid

While cryptocurrency offers exciting opportunities, it also carries risks. Many beginners lose money not because the technology failed — but because they made avoidable mistakes.

Key Risks

- **Volatility:** Prices can rise or fall 20–50% within days. Never invest more than you can afford to lose.
- **Security Threats:** Hacks, phishing attacks, and lost private keys are permanent. Always type official website addresses directly and double-check URLs.
- **Scams & Rug Pulls:** Fraudulent projects lure investors with promises of huge returns, then developers drain the liquidity pool and disappear.
- **Regulatory Uncertainty:** Laws about crypto change rapidly. Some governments ban certain coins or exchanges.
- **Liquidity Risk:** Some tokens cannot be sold quickly due to low trading volume, trapping investors.
- **Ponzi Schemes:** Projects that offer "guaranteed" returns are almost always scams.
- **Social Media Impersonators:** No legitimate project or influencer will ever ask you to send money to get more back.

Security Best Practices

Use Two-Factor Authentication (2FA)

- Always enable 2FA on exchanges and wallets.
- Use an authenticator app (Google Authenticator, Authy) rather than SMS.

Secure Your Private Keys & Seed Phrase

- Write them on paper and store offline.
- Never screenshot or store in email or cloud storage.

Use a Hardware Wallet for Long-Term Storage

- Devices like Ledger or Trezor store crypto offline ("cold storage").

Test Small First

- When sending to a new wallet or exchange, send a small test amount first.

Common Mistakes Beginners Make

- **No DYOR:** Investing based on hype, rumors, or influencer tweets.
- **Chasing Pumps:** Buying when a token is skyrocketing, only to watch it crash.
- **Over-Investing:** Putting rent or savings into crypto without a safety net.
- **Ignoring Fees:** Transaction and withdrawal fees can eat away at small investments.
- **Poor Security:** Leaving funds on exchanges instead of using a secure wallet.
- **FOMO:** Panic-buying or panic-selling based on emotions instead of strategy.

> **The Golden Rule of Crypto**
>
> *"Never invest more than you can afford to lose." Treat cryptocurrency as a high-risk, high-reward asset class — cautious, researched, and measured.*

■ Action Plan — 3 Things You Can Do Today

1. Write down a security checklist: strong passwords, 2FA enabled, hardware wallet purchased.
2. Review your last 3 investments — did you buy based on research or hype?
3. Set a personal investment limit (e.g., max 10% of your portfolio in crypto).

CHAPTER 12

Chapter 12 — Crypto Taxes and Regulations

Crypto is exciting, but it comes with responsibilities — especially taxes and compliance. In most countries, crypto is taxed as property or investment assets.

Common Taxable Events

- Selling crypto for fiat (USD, EUR, etc.).
- Swapping tokens on a DEX.
- Receiving airdrops or staking rewards.
- NFT sales.

Non-Taxable Events

- Buying crypto with fiat (just holding it).
- Transferring between your own wallets.

Tracking Tools

- **CoinTracker:** Syncs with exchanges and wallets; easy gains/loss tracking.
- **Koinly:** Automatic tax reports for multiple countries.
- **CryptoTaxCalculator:** Detailed reporting across DEX and CEX activity.

Capital Gains Basics

- **Short-term gains:** Held less than a year — taxed at regular income rates.
- **Long-term gains:** Held more than a year — may qualify for lower tax rates.
- **Staking, Mining & Yield Farming:** Generally taxed as income when received; may also trigger capital gains when sold.

Global Examples

- **U.S.:** IRS Form 8949 is used to report crypto sales/swaps.
- **U.K.:** HMRC requires records of all crypto disposals, even small ones.
- **Australia:** The ATO has been monitoring exchange activity aggressively since 2021.

Important Disclaimer

Crypto tax laws change quickly, and every country applies different rules. This chapter provides general information, not tax or legal advice. Always consult a licensed tax professional in your jurisdiction before filing.

■ Action Plan — 3 Things You Can Do Today

1. Check your country's rules: search for "crypto taxes [your country]."
2. Download a free version of CoinTracker or Koinly and explore its features.
3. Record today's transactions and start the habit of tracking early.

CHAPTER 13

Chapter 13 — How to Research New Crypto Projects (DYOR Guide)

Do Your Own Research (DYOR) is not just a slogan — it is a survival skill for every investor. The industry is filled with opportunity, but it is also full of hype, scams, and projects that may never deliver.

Step 1: Start With the White Paper

A whitepaper is the project's blueprint. It should explain the problem, the solution, how the technology works, and why the token needs to exist. *Red flag: vague language, buzzwords, or content copied from another project.*

Step 2: Analyze Tokenomics

- **Supply:** How many tokens exist now? What is the maximum supply?
- **Distribution:** Who holds the tokens — early investors, developers, or the community?
- **Utility:** What can you actually do with the token?
- **Inflation/Deflation:** Does supply increase over time or decrease through burning?

Red flag: If a small group controls most of the supply, the risk of "dumping" is high.

Step 3: Evaluate the Team

- **Check identities:** Are founders public (doxxed) or anonymous?
- **Track record:** Have they built successful projects before?
- **Community engagement:** Do they interact with investors on social platforms?

Step 4: Look at the Community

Active, genuine discussions — not just hype or bot activity — signal a healthy project. Overly aggressive promotion or fake followers are red flags.

Step 5: Check for Audits & Security

Has the project undergone an independent code audit? Legitimate projects often reward users for finding flaws (bug bounty programs). *Red flag: no audits, or vague promises of "security coming soon."*

Step 6: Study Market Data

On CoinMarketCap or CoinGecko, review liquidity, trading volume, and price history. A steady growth pattern is more promising than a dramatic pump-and-dump.

Step 7: Use Multiple Sources

- **Social Media:** Twitter (X), Telegram, Discord for updates.
- **News Sites:** Coindesk, The Block, Decrypt.
- **On-Chain Data:** Etherscan, Dune Analytics for transparency.

■ Action Plan — 3 Things You Can Do Today

1. Find a crypto token you want to buy and read its white paper if one exists.
2. Look at its tokenomics on CoinGecko — analyze the supply and distribution.
3. Check the community on Twitter/X, Discord, or Telegram — is it active and genuine?

CHAPTER 14

Chapter 14 — Step-by-Step Walkthroughs for Beginners

This chapter guides you through three essential beginner tasks: setting up a wallet, buying your first token safely, and tracking your portfolio.

Part 1: Setting Up a Wallet

1. **Choose your wallet type –** Hot wallet (app-based): MetaMask or Trust Wallet. Cold wallet (hardware, offline): Ledger or Trezor.
2. **Download from official sources only –** Go to the official website or app store — never click random links.
3. **Install and create your wallet –** Open the app and click “Create New Wallet.”
4. **Back up your recovery phrase –** Write down the 12–24 word seed phrase on paper. Store offline — never on your phone or in email.
5. **Secure with a password –** Use a strong, unique password. Enable biometrics if supported.

Part 2: Buying Your First Token Safely

1. **Choose a trusted exchange –** Coinbase, Binance, or Kraken. Make sure it is regulated in your country.
2. **Verify your identity (KYC) –** Upload ID as required by the platform.
3. **Deposit funds –** Link your bank or card, or transfer stablecoins.
4. **Buy a cryptocurrency –** Start with Bitcoin (BTC) or Ethereum (ETH). Enter the amount you want to purchase.
5. **Transfer to your personal wallet –** Copy your wallet address. Withdraw from the exchange and paste the address carefully. Always test with a small amount first.

Part 3: Tracking Your Portfolio

1. **Install a portfolio tracker –** CoinGecko, CoinMarketCap, Delta, or Blockfolio.

2. **Add your holdings –** Some apps allow automatic syncing; others let you input purchases manually.
3. **Check performance over time –** See gains, losses, and portfolio balance.
4. **Set price alerts –** Get notified when a coin hits your target price.
5. **Review weekly, not hourly –** Avoid emotional decisions from over-checking.

■ Action Plan — 3 Things You Can Do Today

1. Download a hot wallet (e.g., MetaMask) and open a free account on a reputable exchange.
2. Buy $10 worth of a token and transfer it to your wallet.
3. Install a portfolio tracker and add your holdings — then step away for a week.

Appendix — Buying on a CEX and DEX: A Complete How-To Guide

Read This First — Safety Notes

Test with tiny amounts first ($5–$20) before sending large sums. Never share your seed phrase or private keys. Double-check every address and network before sending — blockchain sends are irreversible. Use official apps and URLs only.

A — Buying on Coinbase (CEX)

1. **Create an Account –** Visit coinbase.com or download the Coinbase app. Sign up and have a valid ID ready.
2. **Verify Your Identity –** Submit a government-issued ID to comply with KYC regulations.
3. **Add a Payment Method –** Link a bank account, debit card, or PayPal.
4. **Go to Buy/Sell –** Navigate to the Buy/Sell section and select your cryptocurrency.
5. **Enter the Amount and Confirm –** Specify the amount, review the fee schedule, and confirm the transaction.

B — Set Up Trust Wallet (Mobile)

1. **Download the official app –** Go to trustwallet.com/download. Do not install from search ads.

2. **Create a new wallet** – Tap "Create a new wallet" and accept Terms and Privacy.
3. **Write down your recovery phrase** – Write it on paper and store offline. Never screenshot or store in cloud or phone notes.
4. **Confirm the seed phrase** – The app will ask you to confirm the phrase in order.
5. **Set a passcode/biometrics** – Enable app lock for extra protection.

C — Fund Trust Wallet from Coinbase

For PancakeSwap (BNB Chain) you need BNB on BNB Smart Chain (BEP-20). For Uniswap you need ETH (ERC-20). Sending to the wrong chain will lose funds.

1. **Open Trust Wallet** – Select the token and tap Receive. Copy the wallet address.
2. **On Coinbase** – Go to Send/Withdraw/Transfer. Choose the same asset, paste the Trust Wallet address, select the correct network, and confirm with 2FA.
3. **Wait for confirmations** – Tokens will appear in Trust Wallet after blockchain confirmations.

D — Buying on PancakeSwap (BNB Chain)

1. **Open Trust Wallet** – Go to the DApps or Browser tab. Use WalletConnect if the DApp browser is hidden.
2. **Go to pancakeswap.finance** – Click Launch App, then Connect Wallet → Trust Wallet. Confirm in Trust Wallet.
3. **Select the swap pair** – From: BNB. To: the token you want. Paste the contract address from an official source if not listed.
4. **Set slippage tolerance** – For liquid tokens use 0.5–1%; for new/meme tokens you may need higher.

5. **Approve and swap –** Approve the token first (costs a small gas fee), then click Swap. Confirm in Trust Wallet.
6. **Add custom token if needed –** Tap Add Token → Custom Token → paste the contract address → select BNB Smart Chain.

E — Buying on Uniswap (Ethereum)

1. **Install MetaMask –** Download from the official site and set it up with a seed phrase backup. Or use Trust Wallet + WalletConnect on mobile.
2. **Fund your wallet with ETH –** Via Coinbase → Send. Use the Ethereum (ERC-20) network.
3. **Go to uniswap.org –** Click Launch App → Connect Wallet (MetaMask/WalletConnect).
4. **Choose tokens –** From: ETH. To: the ERC-20 token or paste contract address from an official source.
5. **Set slippage tolerance –** Uniswap default is 0.1%; increase if the token is volatile.
6. **Approve and swap –** Pay an Approve transaction if needed, then confirm the Swap and pay the Ethereum gas fee.
7. **See the token in wallet –** Add custom token if necessary by pasting the contract address.

F — Security & Troubleshooting Checklist

- Always paste addresses (do not type) and confirm the first and last 4–6 characters match.
- Verify contract addresses only from official channels — project website, official Twitter/X.
- If a swap fails: check slippage, token liquidity, gas fees, and transfer taxes or anti-bot measures.

- Keep some native token for gas: BNB for PancakeSwap (BEP-20) and ETH for Uniswap (ERC-20).
- Use small test trades before moving large sums.
- For large holdings, transfer the majority to a cold (hardware) wallet.

Glossary of Cryptocurrency Terms

Address
A unique string of characters used to receive cryptocurrency transactions. Similar to a bank account number, but for the crypto world.

Airdrop
The free distribution of cryptocurrency tokens to multiple wallet addresses, often used as a marketing or community-building strategy.

Altcoins
Any cryptocurrency other than Bitcoin. Created as alternatives, many focus on faster transactions, new features, or specific use cases.

All-Time High (ATH) / All-Time Low (ATL)
The highest or lowest price that an asset has ever reached in its history.

Bear Market / Bull Market
Bear market: prices decline and sentiment is negative. Bull market: prices rise and sentiment is optimistic.

Block
A unit of data on the blockchain that stores transactions. Once added, it becomes a permanent record.

Blockchain
A decentralized digital ledger of transactions, organized into cryptographically linked blocks, ensuring transparency and security.

Burning
Permanently removing tokens from circulation to reduce supply, often intended to increase value.

Centralized Exchange (CEX)
A crypto exchange run by a company or central authority. Examples: Coinbase, Binance.

Cold Wallet
An offline cryptocurrency wallet not connected to the internet. Provides stronger protection from hacks compared to hot wallets.

Consensus Mechanism
The method by which blockchain participants agree on the state of the ledger. Examples: Proof of Work (PoW) and Proof of Stake (PoS).

Contract Address
A unique code identifying a token or smart contract on a blockchain.

Cryptocurrency
A digital or virtual currency that uses cryptography for security and typically operates independently of governments and banks.

Cryptography
The practice of securing information through codes and algorithms. In blockchain, it ensures privacy, authenticity, and integrity.

dApp (Decentralized Application)
An app that runs on a blockchain or decentralized network rather than a centralized server.

DeFi (Decentralized Finance)
Blockchain-based financial applications (like lending, borrowing, or trading) that do not rely on banks or traditional intermediaries.

DEX (Decentralized Exchange)
A peer-to-peer exchange where users trade directly without a central authority.

Doxxed

When a person's real-world identity is publicly disclosed — in crypto, often refers to project founders who have chosen to make their identities known.

Ethereum
A blockchain platform for creating smart contracts and decentralized apps (dApps). Its native currency is Ether (ETH).

Fiat Currency
Government-issued money not backed by a physical commodity (e.g., USD, Euro).

Fork
A split in a blockchain when rules or protocols change. Soft fork: backward-compatible. Hard fork: not backward-compatible.

Gas Fees
Transaction fees on Ethereum and similar blockchains, paid to miners or validators for processing activity.

Governance Token
A cryptocurrency that gives holders voting rights in project decisions.

Hash
A unique string of numbers and letters generated by algorithms to represent data securely.

ICO (Initial Coin Offering)
A fundraising event where new cryptocurrencies are sold to investors, usually in exchange for Bitcoin or Ethereum.

Liquidity
How easily a cryptocurrency can be exchanged for cash or other assets without affecting its price.

Liquidity Pool

Funds locked in a smart contract on a DEX, used to facilitate trading and provide liquidity.

Market Cap (Market Capitalization)

The total value of a cryptocurrency. Formula: circulating supply × current price.

Mining

The process of validating transactions and adding them to the blockchain (in Proof of Work). Miners earn cryptocurrency as a reward.

NFT (Non-Fungible Token)

A unique digital asset stored on a blockchain, often representing art, collectibles, or media. Each is distinct and cannot be replaced.

Node

A computer in the blockchain network that validates transactions and stores data.

Oracle

A service that connects blockchains with real-world data (e.g., price feeds, weather information).

Private Key

A secret code that gives access to your cryptocurrency. Must be kept secure — anyone with it can control your funds.

Proof of Stake (PoS)

A consensus method where validators secure the network by staking tokens. Chosen validators create blocks and earn rewards.

Proof of Work (PoW)

A consensus method where miners solve mathematical puzzles to validate blocks. Requires significant energy.

Public Key

A cryptographic code derived from a private key. Used to receive funds publicly without revealing the private key.

Smart Contract
Self-executing code on a blockchain that automatically carries out an agreement when conditions are met.

Stablecoin
A cryptocurrency pegged to a stable asset (like USD) to minimize volatility.

Token
A digital asset created on a blockchain. Can represent access, ownership, or value within a project.

Tokenomics
The economic model of a cryptocurrency, including supply, distribution, incentives, and utility.

Utility Token
A type of token used to access features, services, or products within a blockchain ecosystem.

Wallet
A tool to store, send, and receive crypto. Hot wallet: internet-connected. Cold wallet: offline.

Whitepaper
A detailed document explaining a cryptocurrency's goals, technology, and roadmap.

Yield Farming
A DeFi strategy where users provide liquidity and earn rewards, interest, or additional tokens.

BONUS: Resource Toolkit

The world of cryptocurrency moves fast. The right tools make the difference between confusion and confidence. Bookmark these and build your own personalized learning flow.

Recommended Wallets

Hot Wallets (Everyday Use):

- **Trust Wallet:** Easy-to-use, mobile-first wallet supporting thousands of tokens and DeFi apps.
- **MetaMask:** The go-to browser extension wallet for Ethereum and EVM-compatible blockchains.
- **Phantom Wallet:** User-friendly, security-minded wallet built for the Solana ecosystem, enabling effortless transactions and Web3 interaction.

Cold Wallets (Long-Term Security):

- **Ledger Nano X:** Hardware wallet for maximum security; integrates with most major blockchains.
- **Trezor Model T:** Open-source hardware wallet, user-friendly with strong community support.

Recommended Exchanges

Centralized (CEX):

- **Coinbase:** Beginner-friendly, easy fiat on/off ramps, strong compliance.
- **Binance:** Largest global exchange, wide token selection, advanced features.
- **Kraken:** Trusted US-based exchange with solid security and fiat support.

Decentralized (DEX):

- **Uniswap:** Leading Ethereum-based exchange; simple and powerful.
- **PancakeSwap:** Popular Binance Smart Chain DEX with low fees.
- **1inch:** DEX aggregator to find the best token swap prices.

Block Explorers

- **Etherscan:** For Ethereum; track tokens, smart contracts, and wallets.
- **BscScan:** For Binance Smart Chain.
- **Blockchain.com Explorer:** For Bitcoin transactions.
- **Solscan:** For Solana network activity.

Education Platforms

- **CoinMarketCap Learn:** Free beginner-friendly guides.
- **CoinGecko Learn & Academy:** Tutorials, glossaries, and market analysis.
- **Binance Academy:** Deep learning library on crypto and blockchain.

Podcasts & YouTube

- **Bankless:** Covers Ethereum, DeFi, and the future of money.
- **Unchained (by Laura Shin):** Expert interviews and big-picture analysis.
- **Coin Bureau (YouTube):** Detailed project breakdowns, tokenomics, and market insights.
- **Whiteboard Crypto (YouTube):** Beginner-friendly animations explaining complex topics.

Portfolio Trackers & Tax Tools

- **CoinStats / Delta / Zerion:** Portfolio trackers that connect wallets and exchanges.
- **Koinly / CoinTracker:** Crypto tax tools with automatic reporting for multiple countries.

Pro Tip

Start small: one hot wallet, one exchange, and one portfolio tracker. Layer in more advanced tools as you grow in confidence.

Crypto Trading Journal

Use the log below to track each trade. Consistent record-keeping helps you identify patterns, learn from mistakes, and stay prepared for tax season.

Date	Buy/Sell	Price	# Tokens	Gain/Loss	Avg Cost

Date	Buy/Sell	Price	# Tokens	Gain/Loss	Avg Cost

Date	Buy/Sell	Price	# Tokens	Gain/Loss	Avg Cost

Date	Buy/Sell	Price	# Tokens	Gain/Loss	Avg Cost

Date	Buy/Sell	Price	# Tokens	Gain/Loss	Avg Cost

Date	Buy/Sell	Price	# Tokens	Gain/Loss	Avg Cost

Date	Buy/Sell	Price	# Tokens	Gain/Loss	Avg Cost

Date	Buy/Sell	Price	# Tokens	Gain/Loss	Avg Cost

Date	Buy/Sell	Price	# Tokens	Gain/Loss	Avg Cost

Date	Buy/Sell	Price	# Tokens	Gain/Loss	Avg Cost

Date	Buy/Sell	Price	# Tokens	Gain/Loss	Avg Cost

Wallet Address Notes

Record your wallet addresses here for easy reference. *Never write your private key or seed phrase in this book* — store those separately in a secure location.

Hot Wallet 1 (e.g., MetaMask / Trust Wallet)

Wallet name / Exchange:

Wallet address:

Notes:

Hot Wallet 2

Wallet name / Exchange:

Wallet address:

Notes:

Cold Wallet (e.g., Ledger / Trezor)

Wallet name / Exchange:

Wallet address:

Notes:

Exchange Wallet 1 (e.g., Coinbase)
Wallet name / Exchange:

Wallet address:

Notes:

Exchange Wallet 2 (e.g., Binance / Kraken)
Wallet name / Exchange:

Wallet address:

Notes:

Additional Addresses & Notes

References

All cryptocurrency statistics and platform information in this book are accurate as of June 2025. The cryptocurrency landscape changes rapidly — always verify current information before acting.

Trusted ongoing resources:

- CoinMarketCap — coinmarketcap.com
- CoinGecko — coingecko.com
- Coindesk — coindesk.com
- Investopedia — investopedia.com
- Ethereum Foundation — ethereum.org
- Bitcoin White Paper — bitcoin.org/bitcoin.pdf
- Nakamoto, S. (2008). *Bitcoin: A Peer-to-Peer Electronic Cash System.*
- NerdWallet Cryptocurrency Investing Guide — nerdwallet.com
- Trust Wallet Official Guides — trustwallet.com/blog/guides
- Coinbase Help Center — help.coinbase.com
- PancakeSwap Documentation — docs.pancakeswap.finance
- Uniswap Documentation — docs.uniswap.org

* * *

The future of cryptocurrency is not just about coins — it is about the transformation of money, assets, and the internet itself. From CBDCs to Web3, tokenization to AI, crypto is laying the foundation for a financial system that is faster, more global, and potentially more inclusive.

Crypto doesn't have to be intimidating. With the right knowledge, you can enter this new financial frontier safely — and even have a little fun along the way.

www.ingramcontent.com/pod-product-compliance
Lightning Source LLC
LaVergne TN
LVHW022314200926
848481LV00004B/1332
* 9 7 8 1 9 4 8 6 1 3 3 5 4 *